MARRIED

Conceptualized and Created by: Latoya Nicole
Illustrations by: Shakira Rivers

ISBN: 979-8-9856190-7-2

For more information, visit us
online at www.entrepreneurscolortoo.com

ENTREPRENEURS
Color
TOO

This book
belongs to:

_____

and....

_____

Getting Started...

This keepsake coloring book includes illustrations of fun and creative ideas that couples can do together like traveling, arts and crafts and skating. The images are across from one another with the intent that you both will color together facing each other. Of course, you can also color at separate times and you'll notice that the first images say "Hubby's side" and "Wifey's side" at the bottom of the page to help get you started. The double blank pages inside are a barrier so that when you color your beautiful creation it has less of a chance of bleeding onto the next image, if you decide to color with markers instead of crayons or colored pencils. Feel free to also doodle on those pages or simply enjoy reading the inspirational quotes listed on wife's side. There are no coloring rules, just have fun creating art together.

May you never forget the love you have for one another.

-Latoya Nicole

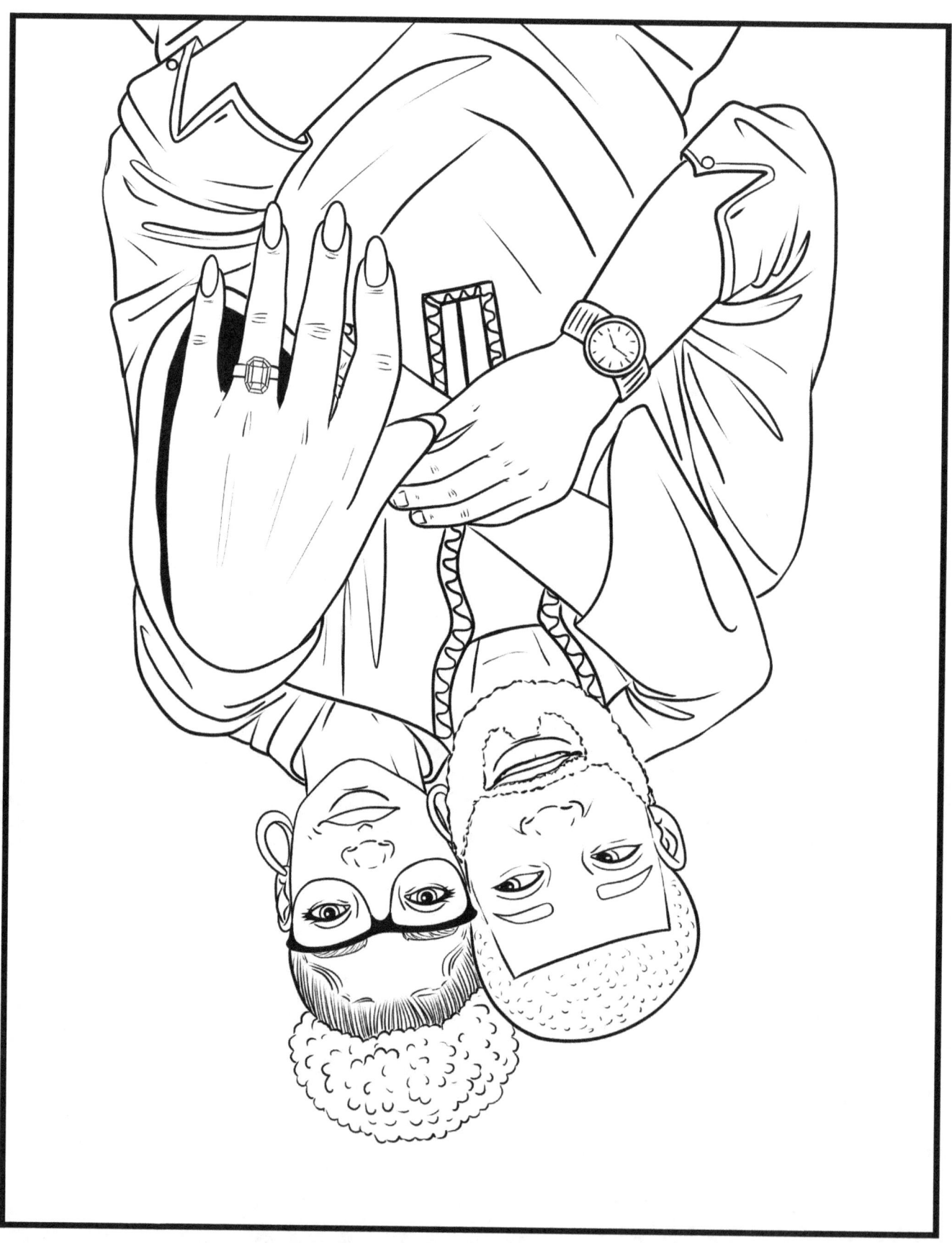

Wifey's Side

Love is patient, love is kind.

There are benefits to keeping some things away from social media.

In case I haven't told you today, I love you.

Your love is a force that knows no bounds, and every moment shared is a victory for both of you.

The love between a husband and wife is forever.

Embrace the journey, for within its twists and turns, you find your strength.

Kindness is the language that connects hearts, spoken by all without words.

I'm proud of many things in life but nothing
beats being a spouse.

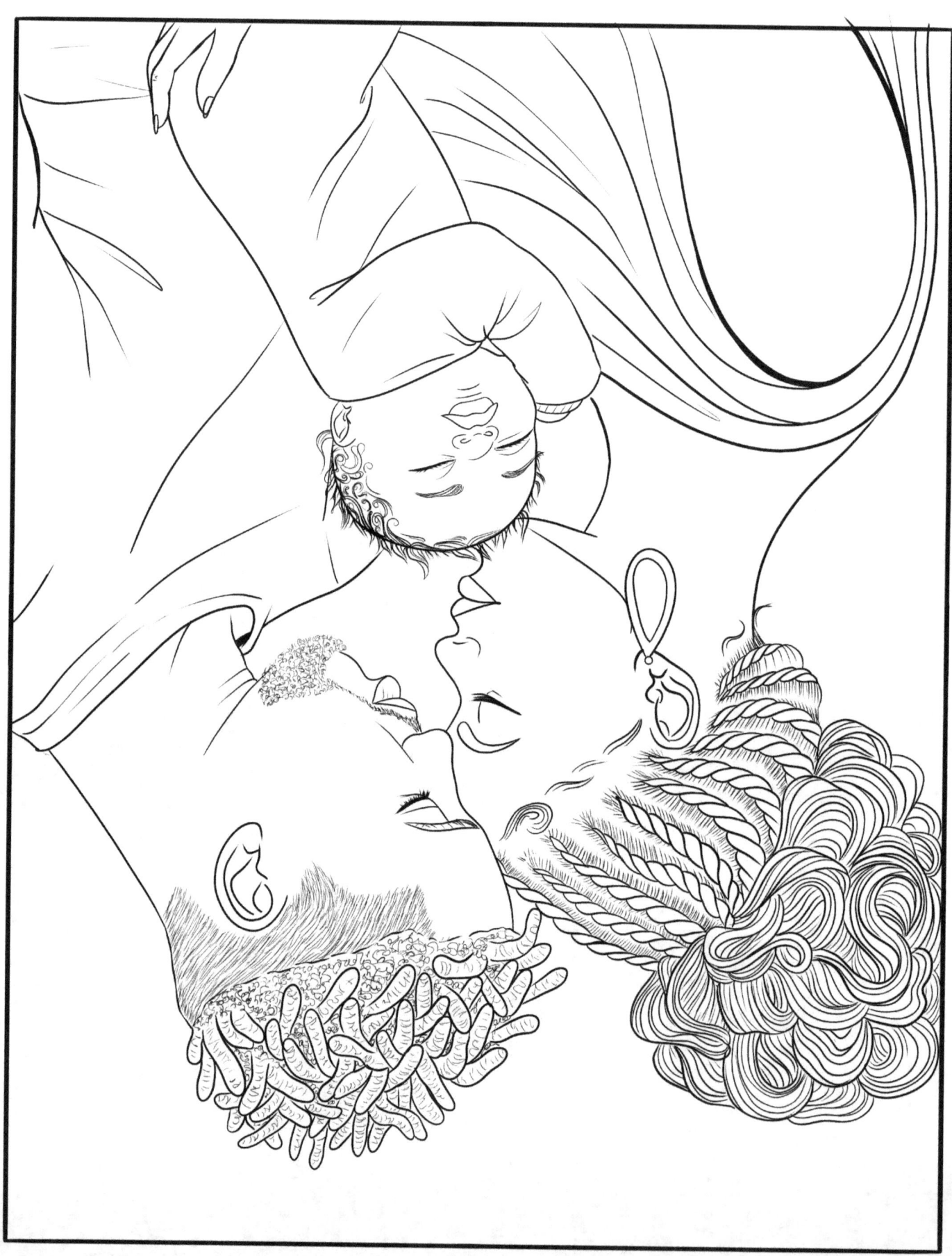

There is nothing as powerful as a bond.

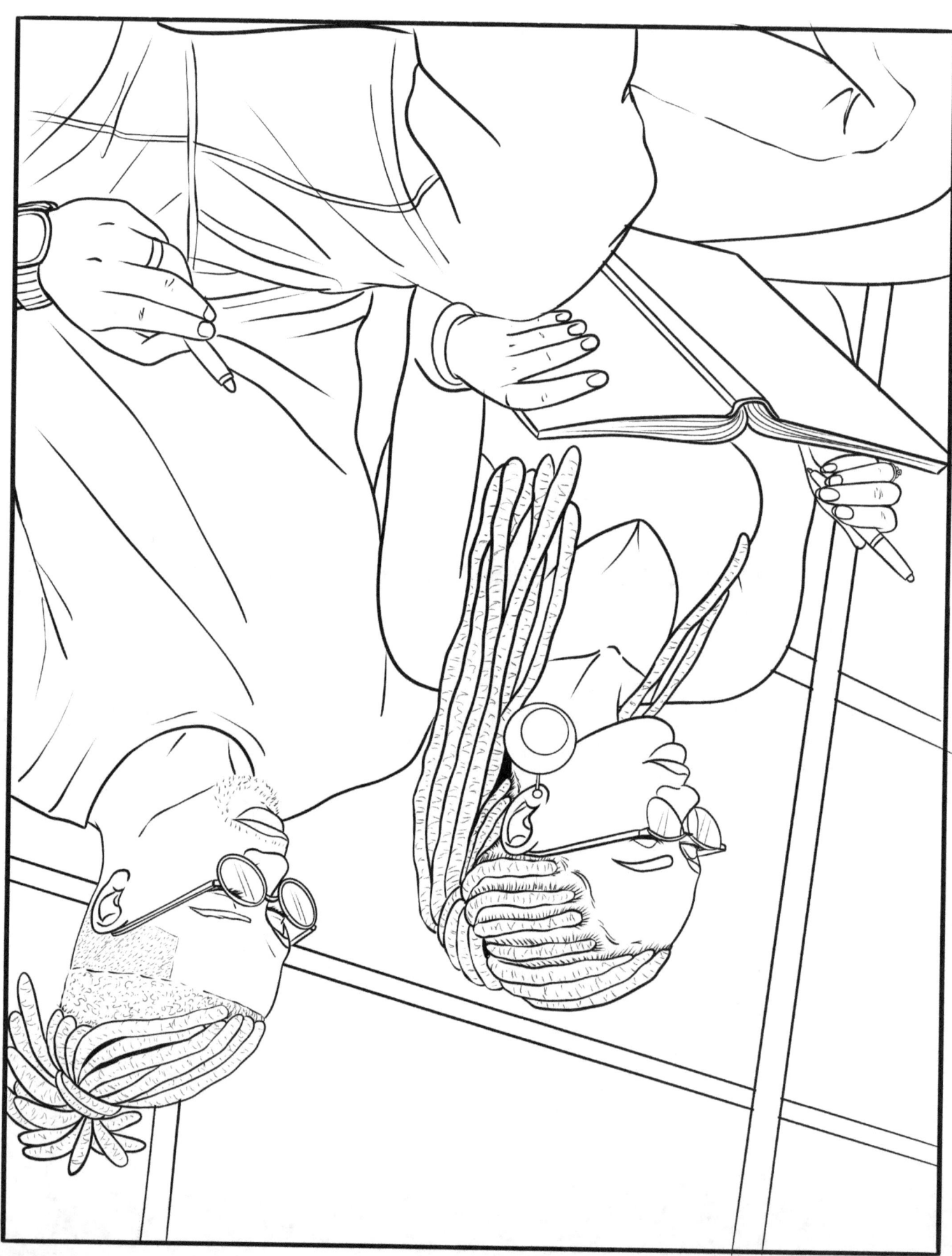

Wisdom is the quiet echo of nature, teaching us to listen before we speak.

Unity is the melody that turns chaos into a harmonious symphony.

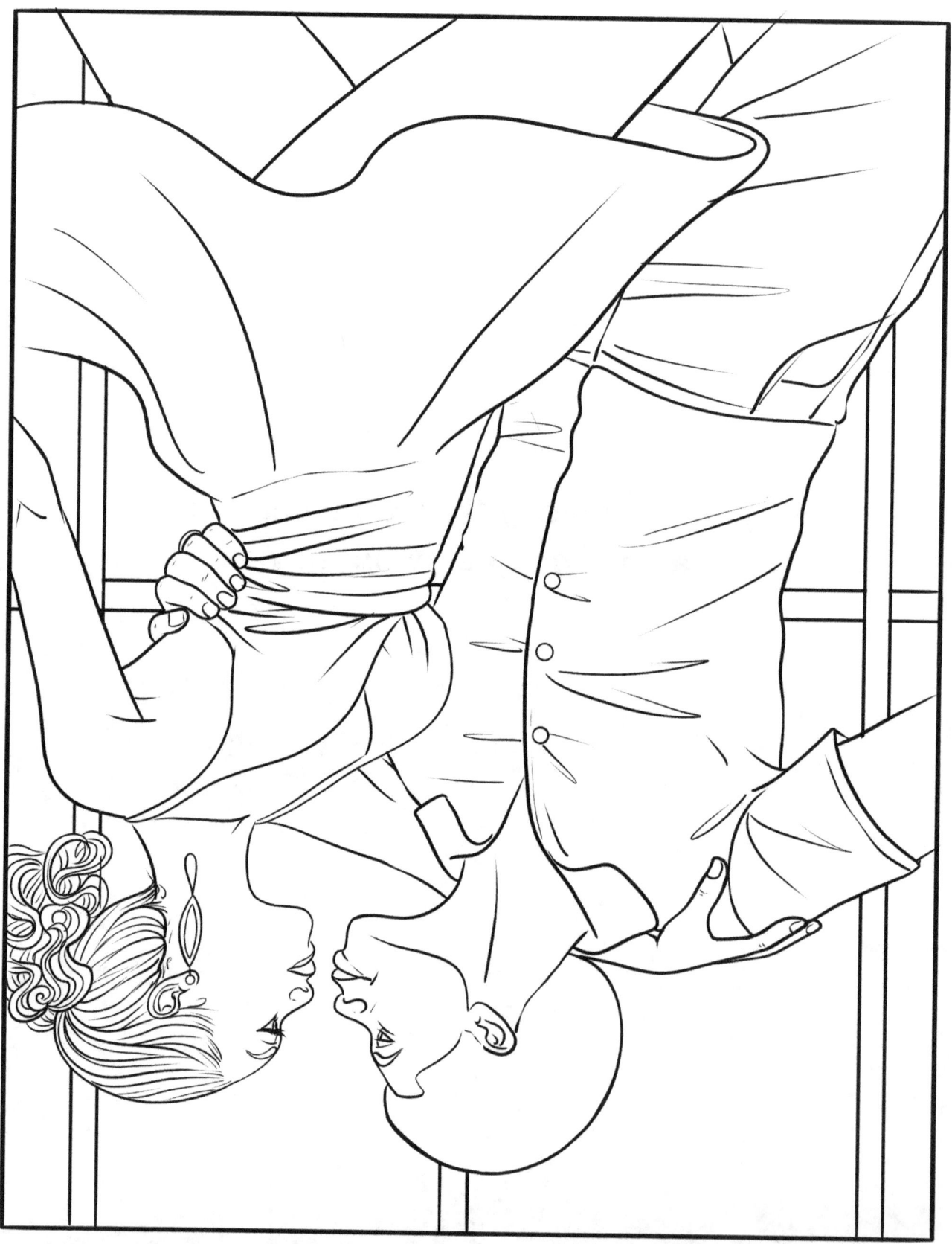

You can accomplish anything your heart desires.